22.49

SUPER COOL FORCES AND MOTION ACTIVITIES with MAX AXIOM

by Agnieszka Biskup

Consultant:
Susan K. Blessing, Ph.D.
Professor of Physics
Director of the Women in Math, Science
and Engineering Program
Department of Physics
Florida State University, Tallahassee

CAPSTONE PRESS
a capstone imprint

...aphic Library is published by Capstone Press,
710 Roe Crest Drive, North Mankato, Minnesota 56003
www.capstonepub.com

Library of Congress Cataloging-in-Publication Data

Cataloging-in-publication information is on file with the Library of Congress.

ISBN 978-1-4914-2079-9 (library binding)
ISBN 978-1-4914-2283-0 (paperback)
ISBN 978-1-4914-2297-7 (eBook PDF)

Editor
Christopher L. Harbo

Art Director
Nathan Gassman

Designer
Tracy McCabe

Production Specialist
Katy LaVigne

Cover Illustration
Marcelo Baez

Project Creation
Sarah Schuette and Marcy Morin

Photographs by Capstone Studio:
Karon Dubke

Printed in the United States of
America in Stevens Point,
Wisconsin.
092014   008479WZS15

Table of Contents

force — any action that changes the movement of an object

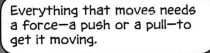

Everything that moves needs a force—a push or a pull—to get it moving.

For instance, pushing away from this platform will get me moving very quickly.

But bungee jumping isn't the only way to experience forces and motion in action. There are tons of awesome activities you can do at home, and I'll show you how.

Get ready to jump into some super cool forces and motion activities!

HARD-BOILED DETECTIVE

Almost 400 years ago, scientist Isaac Newton discovered three simple laws of motion. His first law was the law of **inertia**. It says that an object at rest tends to stay at rest, and an object in motion tends to stay in motion. Use Newton's first law to tell the difference between raw and hard-boiled eggs. You won't even have to crack their shells.

YOU'LL NEED

3 chilled raw eggs

3 chilled hard-boiled eggs

large mixing bowl

1. Carefully place all six eggs in the mixing bowl.

2. Use your hands to gently move the eggs around in the bowl. Be careful not to crack the shells as you mix the eggs.

3. Take the eggs out of the bowl and place them on a smooth, flat surface.

4. Spin each egg on its side.

5. Touch each egg lightly to stop it from moving and then let go immediately.

6. Observe how each egg behaves.

⚡ AXIOM EXPLANATION

Did you notice that some eggs wobbled after you stopped them? Those were the raw eggs demonstrating the law of inertia. When you spun a raw egg, the shell began to move. But the liquid inside the shell did not start spinning as soon as the shell did. Likewise, when you stopped a raw egg, the liquid didn't stop moving right away either. Its movement inside the shell made the egg wobble. A hard-boiled egg's solid center, on the other hand, spun and stopped at the same time as its shell.

inertia—an object's tendency to stay at rest or keep moving at the same speed and in the same direction until a force acts on the object

PENNY DEATH DROP

A resting object's tendency to stay at rest doesn't sound all that exciting. But this super cool coin trick will amaze your friends with the power of inertia.

YOU'LL NEED

- cardstock or other stiff paper
- ruler
- scissors
- tape
- small jar
- water
- penny
- wooden skewer

PLAN OF ACTION

1. Measure and cut a 3/4-inch (2-centimeter) wide by 9 1/2-inch (24-cm) long strip from the piece of cardstock.

2. Form the strip into a hoop and tape the ends together.

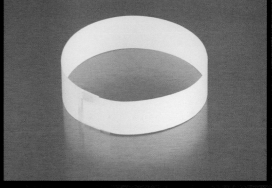

3. Fill the jar with water.

4. Place the hoop vertically on top of the jar.

6. Place the skewer through the center of the hoop and very quickly fling the hoop off to the side.

5. Balance the penny on the top of the hoop, over the center of the jar.

7. Watch where the coin goes.

⚡ AXIOM EXPLANATION

If you flicked the hoop fast enough, the coin landed in the water with a splash. But why didn't the coin follow the hoop across the room? Because the coin has inertia. It's at rest while it sits on top of the hoop. When you flick the hoop, the skewer's forward motion is transferred to the hoop, not the coin. The force of gravity pulls the coin down into the jar.

gravity—a force that pulls objects with mass together; gravity is what pulls objects down toward the center of Earth

MARSHMALLOW CATAPULT

You may not break down castle walls with this marshmallow catapult, but you will see amazing forces in action. Even better, you'll be able to eat your siege machine when you're done with it!

YOU'LL NEED

4 large marshmallows

7 wooden skewers

plastic spoon

tape

rubber band

small candies

PLAN OF ACTION

1. Connect three marshmallows with three skewers to form a triangle. Lay the triangle on a flat surface.

2. Insert one skewer vertically into each marshmallow in the triangle. Angle these three skewers to form a pyramid. Stick the last marshmallow on the point of the pyramid to keep the structure together.

3. Tape the spoon to the end of the remaining skewer.

4. Place the rubber band around the top point of the pyramid.

5. Insert the skewer with the spoon through the rubber band and into one of the marshmallows at the base of the pyramid.

6. Let the catapult sit for at least 24 hours so the marshmallows harden.

7. Place a small candy on the spoon. Gently pull back on the spoon and release to fire the catapult.

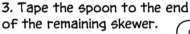

AXIOM EXPLANATION

Newton's second law of motion says that when a force acts on an object, the object's movement will change. The more _____ an object has, the more force it takes to move it. When you pull the catapult's "arm" back and release it, you apply a force to the candy. That force _____ the candy across the room. Newton's second law also says that the greater the force on an object, the greater the change in movement. Pull the catapult's arm back more and less to see Newton's law in action.

mass—the amount of material in an object

accelerate—to change the speed and/or direction of a moving body

BOUNCY BALLS

A tennis ball bounces well on its own. But try teaming it with a basketball. You'll see how **momentum** turns an ordinary bounce into a super one!

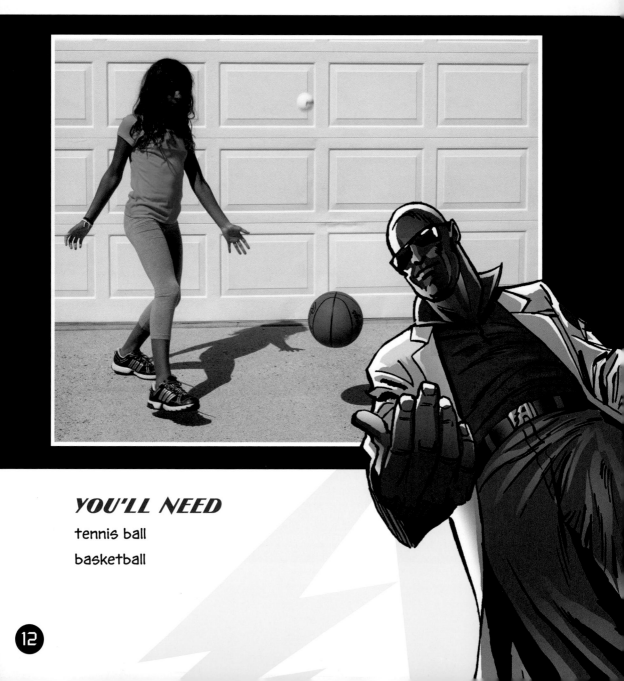

YOU'LL NEED

tennis ball

basketball

PLAN OF ACTION

1. Find an open area of sidewalk or an empty driveway.

2. Drop the tennis ball from shoulder height and see how high it bounces.

3. Drop the basketball from shoulder height and see how high it bounces.

4. Put the tennis ball on top of the basketball, and drop them together from shoulder height again. What happens to the tennis ball?

⚡ AXIOM EXPLANATION

Momentum is the measure of a body's motion. It is equal to the body's mass times its velocity. The basketball has more momentum as it falls because it has more mass than the tennis ball. When the basketball hits the ground, some of that momentum passes into the ground. But the remaining momentum passes to the tennis ball. The tennis ball has less mass than the basketball, which means it will gain a greater velocity. This additional momentum sends the tennis ball soaring.

momentum—the amount of motion an object carries

velocity—the speed and direction of a moving object

BOTTLE BOAT

Some boats are powered by the wind, others by gasoline. To see Newton's third law of motion in action, you'll power a boat using baking soda and vinegar!

YOU'LL NEED

plastic drink bottle with cap

small scrap of wood

small nail

hammer

1 tablespoon (15 mL) of baking soda

5 marbles

4 ounces (125 mL) of vinegar

large tub of water or bathtub

1. Place the bottle's cap on the scrap of wood. Punch a hole in the cap by hammering the nail through it.

2. Place the baking soda inside the bottle.

3. Add marbles to the bottle to weigh it down.

4. Pour in the vinegar and quickly cap the bottle.

5. Tip the bottle so the marbles roll near the cap. Then place the bottle in the tub so the cap is under water.

⚡ AXIOM EXPLANATION

Newton's third law states that for every action, there is an opposite and equal reaction. By actions, Newton meant forces. When vinegar and baking soda mix together, they react and produce carbon dioxide gas. The gas wants to escape through the hole in the cap. The escaping gas pushes against the water and moves the boat forward. The action is the gas rushing out of the hole. The reaction is the boat moving forward.

BALLOON CAR

Rockets use the force of **thrust** to launch into outer space. You'll use the force of thrust to launch a balloon car across the room.

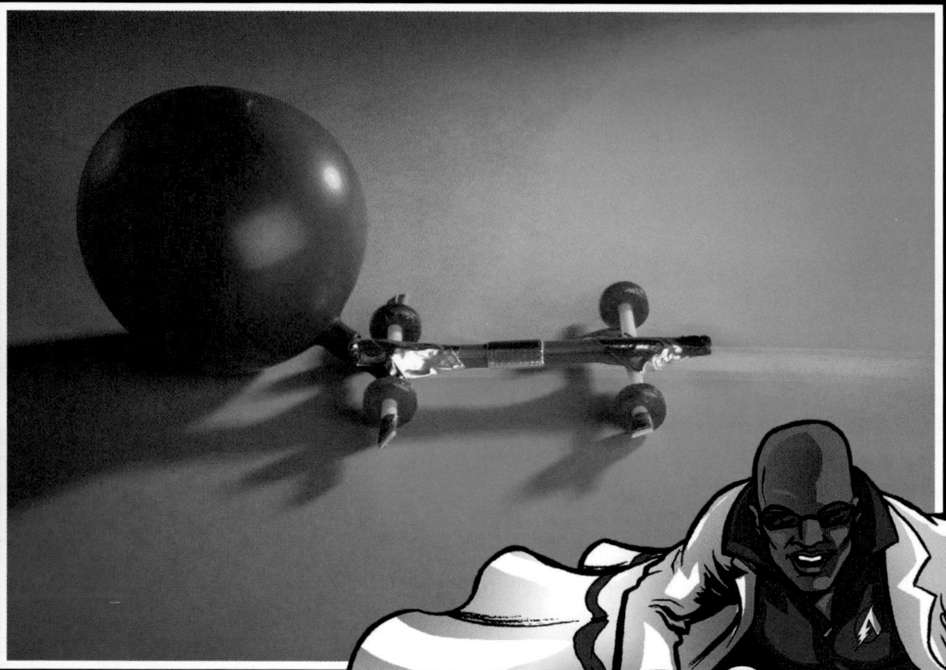

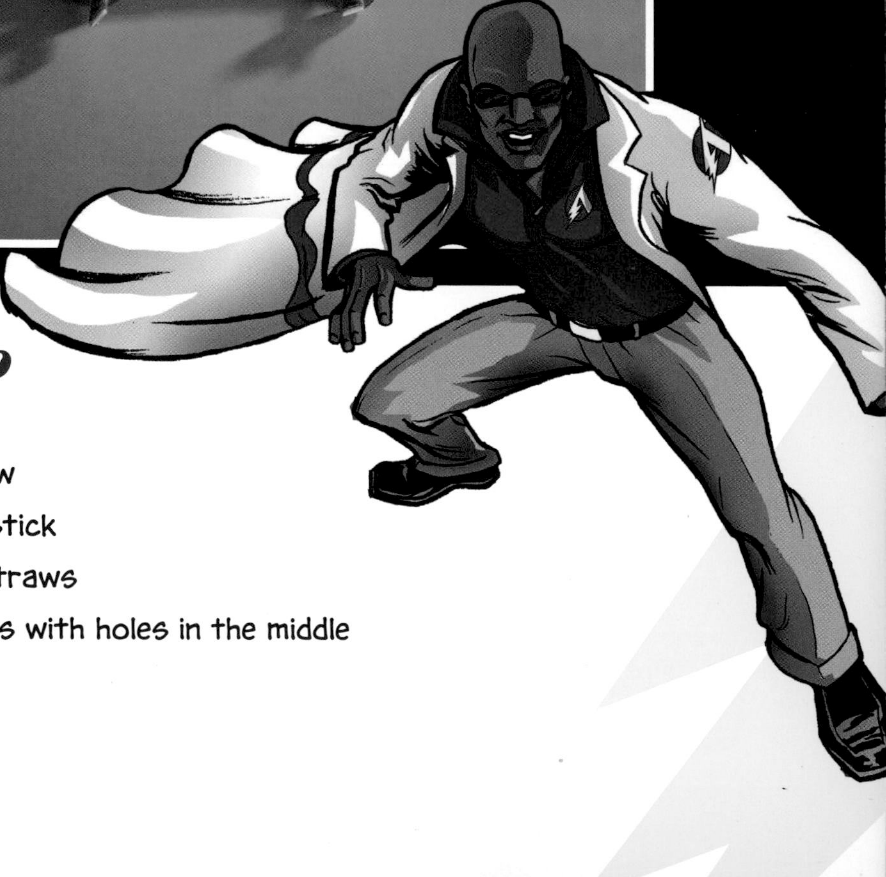

YOU'LL NEED

small balloon

flexible plastic straw

flat wooden craft stick

2 straight plastic straws

4 round hard candies with holes in the middle

tape

2. Seal the mouth of the balloon around the end of the straw with tape.

3. Tape the straw to the top of your flat wooden stick. This is your "jet."

4. Slip two candies onto a straight straw. Bend back and tape the tips of the straw on both ends so the candies can't fall off. Repeat with the second straight straw.

thrust—a force that pushes an object in a given direction

continued

5. Tape the straws with the candies to the bottom of your flat stick. One should be directly below the balloon. These are your "wheels." Make sure they spin freely.

6. Blow up the balloon through the straw. Put your finger over the end of the straw to keep the air from escaping.

7. Place your car on a smooth surface. Adjust the flexible straw so the balloon doesn't touch the surface.

8. Release your finger from the straw and let the car go.

AXIOM EXPLANATION

Newton's third law of motion is at work once again. The balloon's stored air creates thrust that moves the car forward. When the air in the balloon moves in one direction, it pushes the car in the opposite direction. This is the same way that rockets work. A rocket pushes gas out of its engines. Then the gas pushes back on the rocket and lifts it into space.

FRICTION FUN

Why do people and cars slip and slide on ice? The key is **friction**—or the lack of it! See how things move differently when friction is reduced.

YOU'LL NEED

cardboard shoebox without lid

scissors

balloon

masking tape

tape measure

notebook

pencil

box of plastic drinking straws

friction—a force created when two objects rub together; friction slows down objects

continued

PLAN OF ACTION

1. Cut a small hole at one end of the shoebox. Make the hole about two-thirds of the way down from the top of the box.

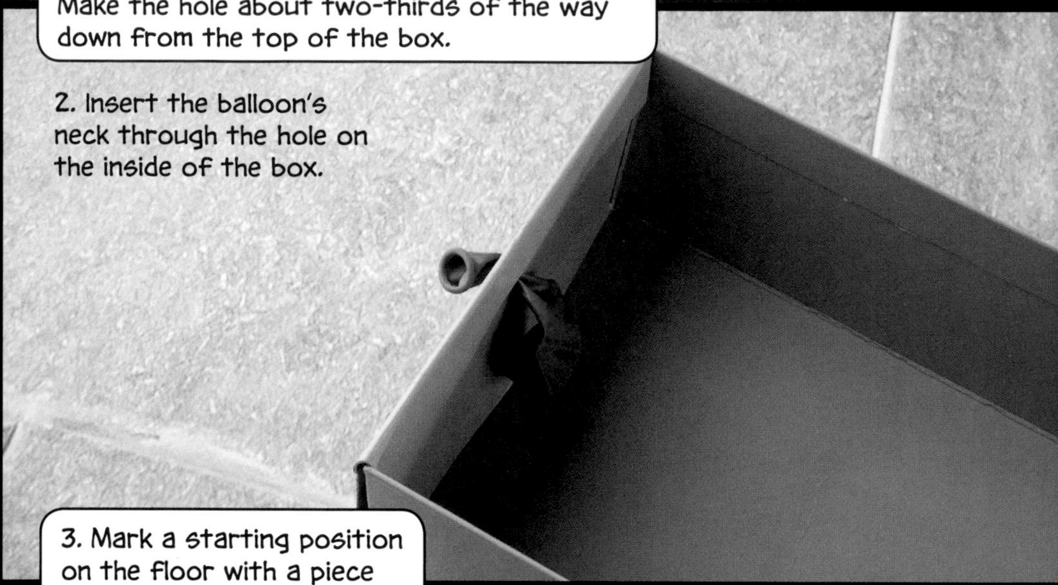

2. Insert the balloon's neck through the hole on the inside of the box.

3. Mark a starting position on the floor with a piece of masking tape.

4. Blow up the balloon and hold it closed with your fingertips.

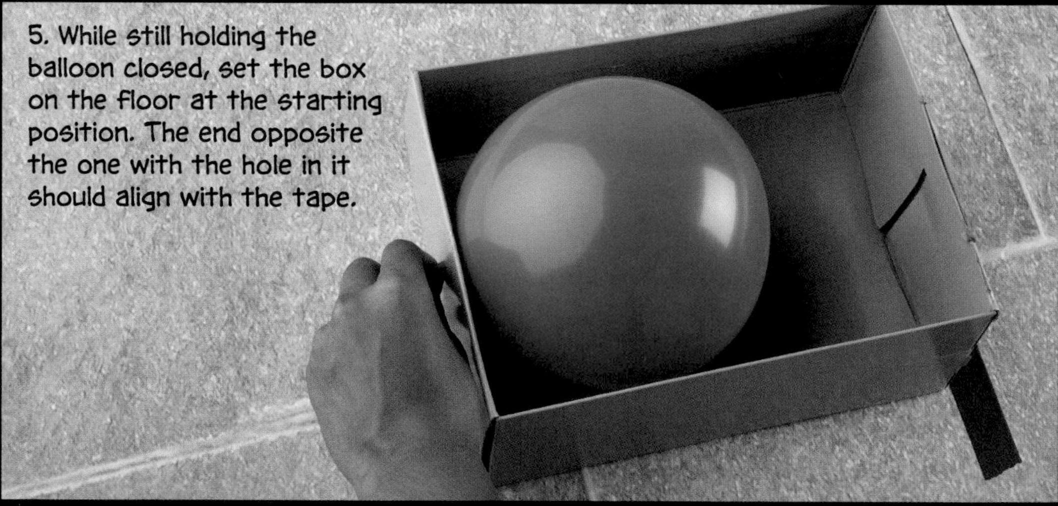

5. While still holding the balloon closed, set the box on the floor at the starting position. The end opposite the one with the hole in it should align with the tape.

6. Let go of the balloon and measure how far the box traveled from the starting point. Write it down in your notebook.

7. Lay out a "runway" of plastic drinking straws about 3 feet (1 meter) in length starting behind the marked starting position.

8. Inflate the balloon in the box, and holding the balloon closed, set the box atop your runway.

9. Release the balloon. Measure how far the box traveled. Write down your result and compare it to the first.

AXIOM EXPLANATION

Any time two objects rub against each other, they cause friction. Friction is a force that works against motion. There are different types of friction. On a flat surface, the box is working against sliding friction. But on the straw runway, the box is working against rolling friction. Rolling friction occurs when a round surface rolls over another surface. Your box overcomes rolling friction much easier than sliding friction, so it should have moved farther on the straw runway.

PING-PONG WATER BOTTLE TRICK

Can you feel the pressure? You don't notice it, but the air around you constantly pushes on your body. Check out the surprising power of **air pressure** with a ping-pong ball and a bottle of water.

YOU'LL NEED

empty glass drink bottle

pitcher of water

plastic tub

ping-pong ball

PLAN OF ACTION

1. Place the glass bottle in the center of the large plastic tub.

2. Fill the bottle with water until it's overflowing.

3. Place the ping-pong ball on the mouth of the bottle. A little water should come out.

4. Pick up the bottle and carefully turn it upside down over the tub.

⚡ AXIOM EXPLANATION

If the force of gravity pulls on the water and the ping-pong ball, why don't they both fall away from the bottle when you turn it upside down? The answer lies in the shape of the ball. It is a sphere with a lot of surface area. The air pressure all around the sphere keeps the ball in place. Ordinary air pressure is 14.7 pounds per square inch (1 kilogram per square centimeter). It provides enough force to keep the ball sealed to the bottle.

air pressure—the weight of air pushing against something; since air is a fluid, the pressure forces push equally in all directions

ARTIFICIAL GRAVITY IN A GLASS

Some amusement parks have a ride called the Gravitron. Riders stand against the inner wall of a giant spinning cylinder while the floor drops out. The spinning motion keeps the riders glued against the wall without them slipping down. You can create your own mini artificial-gravity ride using a glass and a marble.

YOU'LL NEED

smooth-sided beverage glass

marble

1. Hold the glass upright by gripping its flat base with one hand.

2. Place the marble in the bottom of the glass.

4. While still swirling the glass, tilt it on its side. The marble should continue spinning in a circle.

3. Start swirling the glass so that the marble moves in a circle.

5. Turn the glass upside down as you continue swirling.

⚡ AXIOM EXPLANATION

On a very tiny scale, you've just created artificial gravity! The force that keeps the marble moving in a circle is called *centripetal force*. Any object in motion tends to stay in motion in a straight line, unless something gets in its way. In this case, the curved shape of the glass makes the marble change direction. At the same time, the friction between the marble and the glass prevents the marble from falling.

centripetal force—the force that pulls an object turning in a circle inward toward the center

GOING MARBLES

Centripetal force keeps you in your seat when you go upside down on a roller coaster. It gives you a push when you're inside a car that's turning quickly. It even keeps satellites from falling out of the sky. But to see actual evidence of this invisible force, all you need is a marble and some gelatin.

YOU'LL NEED

2 clear plastic cups

one-hole paper puncher

duct tape

18 inches (46 cm) of string

pot

measuring cup

1 package of cherry gelatin

1 package of lemon gelatin

marble

flashlight

SAFETY FIRST

Ask an adult to help you make the gelatin because you'll need boiling water.

PLAN OF ACTION

1. Make a hole about 1 inch (2.5 cm) from the top rim of a plastic cup with the paper puncher. Make a second hole directly opposite from the first hole.

2. Stick small pieces of duct tape over the edge of the cup above each hole. The tape should extend to, but not cover, the holes.

3. Thread the string through the holes and tie the ends securely to the edge of the cup.

4. Follow the directions on the package to make the lemon gelatin.

5. Fill the unused plastic cup about halfway full with the lemon gelatin.

continued

6. Place the cup in the referigerator for about four hours so that the gelatin sets.

7. Remove the cup from the refrigerator and gently press a marble into the gelatin. Allow half of the marble to remain above the gelatin's surface.

8. Follow the directions on the package to make the cherry gelatin. Carefully pour this mixture on top of the lemon gelatin. Leave about 1 inch (2.5 cm) of space at the top of the cup.

9. Place the cup back in the refrigerator for another four hours, until the cherry gelatin is completely set.

10. Remove the cup from the refrigerator and stack it inside the cup with the string attached.

11. Find an open area outside. Hold the string handle and swing the stacked cups quickly for 20 complete revolutions next to your body. Make sure you make a complete circle each time.

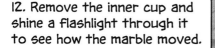

12. Remove the inner cup and shine a flashlight through it to see how the marble moved.

⚡ AXIOM EXPLANATION

The marble should have moved to the bottom of the cup. While the contents of the cup "want" to move in a straight line, the cup pushes them inward. The tension in the string provides the centripetal force on the cup, and the cup provides the centripetal force on the gelatin. Since the gelatin isn't completely solid, the marble moves through it until it reaches the bottom of the cup. This is the same force that keeps you firmly in your seat when you're upside down in a loop on a roller coaster.

Glossary

accelerate (ak-SEL-uhr-ate)—to change the speed and/or direction of a moving body

air pressure (AIR PRESH-ur)—the weight of air pushing against something; because air is a fluid, the pressure forces push equally in all directions

centripetal force (sen-TRI-puh-tuhl FORS)—the force that pulls an object turning in a circle inward toward the center

force (FORS)—any action that changes the movement of an object

friction (FRIK-shuhn)—a force created when two objects rub together; friction slows down objects

gravity (GRAV-uh-tee)—a force that pulls objects with mass together; gravity is what pulls objects down toward the center of Earth

inertia (in-UR-shuh)—an object's tendency to stay at rest or keep moving at the same speed and in the same direction until a force acts on the object

mass (MASS)—the amount of material in an object

momentum (moh-MEN-tuhm)—the amount of motion an object carries

thrust (THRUHST)—a force that pushes an object in a given direction

velocity (vuh-LOSS-uh-tee)—the speed and direction of a moving object

Read More

Coupe, Robert. *Force and Motion*. Discovery Education: How It Works. New York: PowerKids Press, 2014.

Mercer, Bobby. *Junk Drawer Physics: 50 Awesome Experiments that Don't Cost a Thing*. Chicago: Chicago Review Press, Inc. 2014.

Weakland, Mark. *Thud!: Wile E. Coyote Experiments with Forces and Motion*. Warner Bros. Wile E. Coyote, Physical Science Genius. North Mankato, Minn.: Capstone Press, 2014.

Internet Sites

FactHound offers a safe, fun way to find Internet sites related to this book. All of the sites on FactHound have been researched by our staff.

Here's all you do:

Visit *www.facthound.com*

Type in this code: 9781491420799

Super-cool stuff!

Check out projects, games and lots more at
www.capstonekids.com

Index